The Sunken Lightship

THE SUNKEN LIGHTSHIP

POEMS

PETER MAKUCK

BOA EDITIONS, LTD. / BROCKPORT, NY, 14420 / 1990

ISBN: 0–918526–74–4 Cloth
        0–918526–75–2 Paper

LC #: 89–82682
First Edition

Publications by BOA Editions, Ltd.
are made possible with the assistance of grants from
the Literature Program of the New York State Council on the Arts
and the Literature Program of the National Endowment for the Arts,
as well as with financial assistance from private foundations,
corporations and individuals.
BOA Editions, Ltd. is a non-profit literary organization.

Cover Photo: Ray Scharf
Cover Design: Daphne Poulin
BOA Logo: Mirko

Typesetting: Sans Serif, Inc.
Manufacturing: MacNaughton & Gunn, Lithographers

BOA Editions, Ltd.
A. Poulin, Jr., President
92 Park Avenue
Brockport, NY 14420

CONTENTS

for Phyllis and Keith

The Sunken Lightship

I

DARK PREFACE

The blind—
They're barely noticed
Unless, as today, I see one
Nearly hit by a car; he freezes, then moves again,
A kind of sleep stumble, following secret
Footage in the skull. His cane whispers
Through leaves on the walk—whispers
I follow at a distance, almost afraid
Of the eyepits, the face tilted back
As if searching
For something gone from the sky.
He shuffles past deafening rock and the blank
Of frat house windows.
On a dark street, I watch him disappear
Into a darkened house,
The light unexpected

Yellow as forsythia
That borders my parents' back porch
Where my deaf cousin and his signing friends
Are waiting for beer.
I pause at the door.
Delight creases their cheeks.
Words fill the eyes. Hands
Ballet; fingers fold and open, circle,
Figure the air and make it mean
Something funny this time. They laugh
A laughter so pure, you're listening
To nothing but light.

STORY OF A SOUND

It begins in the vestry
With a customary two dollar bill
From groom to servers.
    My first wedding,
A scent of wine from cut glass cruets—
The same burgundy
Color as the kneeler cushions
Where they wait for their names
From the priest:
"Dominic Trancreda . . . Carmella Peronne...."

Her bridal veil is lifted,
A small yellow stain on the bodice,
The face pale,
A beauty mark above her parted lips . . .
"Do you, Carmella, take...."
Looking at me, she lowers her eyes,
And the silence stretches to a yes.

That night, the newspaper says
Her husband, a dent in the middle
Of his heavy chin, is a butcher.
I clip her photo, carry her heart-
Shaped face for months
Behind the veil,
As if in a cocoon,
Lips the color of a cherry
That tops the sundae
I'm famished for. Then, whispering
Carmella, Carmella,
I taste the sound
That deepens everything I see.

She wants
To live a certain kind of life
Away from the block and cleaver,
The hateful apron smeared with red,
Her voice urging,
Do it for me, Carmella,
That name in the nightroom turning
The barrel of a portrait lens—
Carmella at the altar of sleep
Lovelier than any madonna,
Giving her name to my lips
Even when awake.

Carmella.
I'm twelve,
Married for the first time
To a name.

ANSWERING VOICES

We address an emptiness in the street
Or in the mute space of a journal,
Puzzling with the sounds that we hear.
Inside is where they sleep
Or come at waking
From a sphere we barely believe in.
Angels of welcome,
They beg for response,
Invite a self to sound itself out.

Imperative, they throb into being,
The language as plain as a mother's:
Shhh, your father's asleep.
Or the nearly forgotten
Pitch and rhythm of an old priest:
Pater noster qui es in caelis. . . .
Dead language
Brought back to life.
And we have answered the angels.

Lips moving, caught in the act,
Our faces crimson, still
We carry on with punch-lines,
Bookish abstractions,
The vulgate figures of friends,
Whatever serves
This odd process of oxygenation,
A motion that carries toxin from the blood,
Inflates the half-filled lung.

A moon floats over the trees,
Round and bright as a new Spalding:
Fork your fingers on the stitches.
It's my uncle's voice,
Ragged with tobacco and vodka.
Alone, we are never alone.

BROTHERS OF THE DOUBLE LIFE

Love is basically a suspension of gravity.
                              —DON DeLILLO

Against the wind and rain, the house
Makes odd sounds as if trying to be still.
The invisible is all around us, you once joked,
But thin air has been your home
For nearly a year.

Air, even and steady, a bright chain rising
From the tiny diver in my son's aquarium, safe
From the stormy light that makes
Everything something else—those pillows
A body, that shoe a rat.
      The aquarium glows,
A calm green lamp of magnification.

Today, small craft warnings
And to be out at the reef would be a bad dream,
But in other weather, gung-ho for grouper,
We drifted live bait from first light,
      From reef to the tanker wreck.
And the Carolina coast showed off
As if it knew you were from up north
And didn't have long
To take in the fantasia of pink and pearl clouds
And April fragrance
      That the land breathed out all morning.

Makos often fin the wreck
    But this day it was dolphin,
Eyes so keen, they were in
    And out of our lines,
Playing, without ever grazing a bait,
Or causing a reel to click even once,
Water clear to fifty feet down
Where, half-hidden by its white-spotted mama,
A calf synchronized its swimming to hers.

Never had I seen so many this close.
As if needed, here they were,
Come to the rescue, near enough to pet,
You leaning over the bow, dipping a hand
As if such water could cure
Divorce, lost children, parents recently dead.
But watching was enough,
The quick caper and flurry
That elongates and launches those great smilers
High in the air where they hang
Before becoming wholly water again.

Perfect, like the clarity
Of my son's aquarium, where lyre-tail,
Pearl and pink gourami
Slowly turn, or hang weightless as dreams—
A reminder of what you never were,
Weightless, always running, biking,
Training your body to be less and less.
And now it's gone, it's air
Like the dolphin you leaned toward,
Just out of reach, untouchable,

Mysterious as the future,
The dolphin I count on
To swim me asleep.

Waterlight ripples on the white plaster wall.
The invisible presses
With a lowering sky,
    The line squall that drove us into port
Then home along a rainy road,
    Still seeing those dolphin,
Yet unequal to what we saw,
Reduced to a beer and a wise joke
About how we would never again take the bait.

But more like sharks than dolphin,
We do take the bait, move forward to breathe,
The dead living in us
As we breathe them into a future
Of perfect moments, like this one
Before the aquarium that reminds us
Of radiance and grace.
We watch from the world of air,
Haunted by the green inner calm,
Always hoping it will dream us again.

In memory of Bernard Meredith

⌐—,

FEEDERS

My father
To feed us
Was stuck in shiftwork
Lost to the sun
And moon for years.
My mother,
As she put it,
Was stuck in the sticks
But learned to make
Each one matter.
To stay alive
She fed the birds
And squirrels,
Brought them
To the window feeder
Crumb by crumb.
Even the crows.
Slowly, patiently,
She made a family
Of ducks
Come from the pond
To the back door.
With a soft voice
She coaxed
The small life close,
Showing me
That the wild,
Like the poor,
We must keep
Always with us.

CATLIGHT

There is so little that is close and warm.
                              —WALLACE STEVENS

Cats won't perform.
        They make *you* perform.
So here you are, playing
        Master of the Back Door,
Powerless, feeling the winter
        Freeze and the dark
That suggests—but just then
        A touch of white.

From the dark depths,
        In no hurry, she comes,
Nonchalant across the lawn,
        Under the car,
Stopping to scratch an ear,
        Then sits and stares,
While you attend the door
        And babytalk
To the backyard until she decides
        It's time.

Nose still wet and cold, she
        Presents herself
To your lap, the gift she knows
        You know she is,
And takes you from trivia,
        TV news, some article
You recall about cats
        Spending two thirds
Of their lives asleep, or at rest.

Your fingers, drunk on her fur,
    Forget that tabled wineglass
And slip over the patchwork of black,
    White, and the rust
That turns to *café au lait* when you pet
    Against the grain.

And the exquisite whiskers, her skull
    Like a kneecap, that mouth,
Like a snake's when she yawns,
    Which is often,
Then the tickling rasp of her tongue.

Drowsing, she purrs her one mantra
    While the left ear
Independently tracks a kid
    Peeling rubber in the street.
Her one cracked eye is a vote
    For dynamic stillness.

    Yes, you say, and mumble
About Eastern Thought, immobility,
    Pascal and *divertissement*.

But like one of your students,
    She yawns again,
For you're such a slow learner—
    She's so tired
Of teaching you stillness,
    Nonchalance,
How to care while seeming not to,
    Sleeping
So that you might,
    As in rare moments like this,
Dream wide awake,
    Making all things live
In vivid, unusual light, catlight.

AFTER FRIENDS

Past beersmell and smoke, faces
Like party balloons,

Spring-groan and door-slap: this is the way
To the wooden back porch:

Slow clouds, black spaces, quiet—
All come to the bottom stair.

The tongue buds open to a last inch of wine.
A breeze starts up.

And in the forgotten hibachi, like desire
Strawberries suddenly ripen.

⸺

WITH MY FATHER
AT CROW'S NEST COTTAGE

Small craft warnings.
A carp flag in tatters
On the cottage pole.

I made him hold on
To my arm and
Walk the soft sand
For his own good.

He stopped
And I stepped back
For a moment
To take this picture—
His eyes wrinkled
Like the endangered
Loggerhead turtles
In the dunes.
But it was a double-
Exposure: me
Watching him
Earlier that week,
As he entered the water
On stick legs,
Get smaller
And smaller
Until I thought
He would vanish
Completely.

That camera was
A box made of my fingers
To make us laugh—
And it worked.

Today I picture him
Still standing on his own,
Back to the toppling waves,
In a slicker burning
Blue as the moment,
Managing to laugh,
Giving form to the infinite
Depth of field
At his back.

A SENSE OF THE OTHER SIDE

Back home at last
After seeing my mother
Lowered into frozen earth,
I couldn't find sleep
With wine or even pills,
When our calico, as if
Called, came to the sofa
And did something
Never repeated since—

One soft foot at a time,
She climbed on my chest,
Looked through the blank
Lid of my face, made
The faintest cry, then
Curled over my heart
And slept, so that I could,
For three nights in a row—
Visitations like belief,
Unreal, against all odds.

—

BACKWATERS

From behind, out of nowhere,
Two bass boats in a race rocket by,
Their big Mercs at throat-open roar—
Roostertail fallout and a wake
Tall enough to spill over my gunnels.

So I lean on the oars and ease out of propwash,
The sullen swirls of the boat-crowded river
Into the glass backwaters
Of Tranter's Creek.

All meanders,
This is the right place for reflection.
At least two of everything.
And hard to tell which birch is real
Until a mullet, lacing back and forth, wobbles
The deep black mirror.

Everything so much the same
I could blink and be two years back,
And my father, astonished, might still point
    To the ghost-blue heron,
    Thin-shouldered and stalking,
    Solemn as a monk,
As I drift in this dory,
    The last of my father's gifts.

A squirrel barks, then barks again.

Two years, day after day.
Tree, branch, twig—everything repeats itself.
Even his voice, a scratch of dry leaves at the end.
Crows tow the season back into place,
This place,
Where the ear will take you further than ever.

In moments like this, I half expect
That dead oak to speak from its bird-hole.
Yet nothing happens. Then happens again.
The snap of a twig
Footsteps moving toward the bank.

If I'm right, my father's here
And the air is full of him trying to speak.

EQUATIONS

The lights flicker and the kitchen
Disappears until my mother comes back
With a hurricane lamp, determined
That a blackout won't keep me from homework.

Everything is still but the wind
And the steady gas breath of the oven
Where the bread keeps rising,
The scent of yeast and nutmeg spreading.

My father is at work in the shipyard,
And every school night of this rainy winter
In the year of Sister Scholastica's scowl
My mother helps me with impossible math.

Let x equal the moment
That the power fails, as if Germans
Have zeroed in on the light above tabled books
And my mother's selfless ambitions.

And y the way space shrinks
And draws so comfortably close
That the shove and slug of the playground
Disappear with the granite church:

x plus y plus the bright water
Of her eyes where I see myself
Suspended, dark and tiny, but in fine detail,
Held intact, ready at last to respond.

SAILPLANE

Tonight we test what I've taught him,
Carry our week's worth of gluing through
A maze of streets to the stadium, top tier,
The only place with height enough.

We launch into a falling dark,
My cousin a week dead, just a kid, killed
By a junkie she had seen rob a store.

The sun is down, the sky is losing its red
To the big white wings that teeter on small drafts,
Slide out above the empty seats,
Bank and glide toward the pale gates of the endzone.

Evening deepens its tones.
Remember, don't touch his arm too much,
Instruct too much.
Allow him to fly it himself,
Again and again a white cross
Soon disappearing after sixty feet.
Wait. Watch him vanish, return and vanish.

Nighthawks swerve for bugs.
A Harley attacks the distance on Highway 51.

When we leave, he carries the wings.
I carry the body. The moon comes up.
Our plane has put a hole in the dark
That is afterwards darker,
Wings of the sailplane whiter.

STEPHEN JUDY'S EXECUTION

His face fills the screen,
Famous a little longer for its smile
And canine teeth, big like mine.

He looks beyond the camera
At all the late-night drinkers and snackers,
Without remorse, determined to die.

Pitiless, he smiles.
Cut to a room, all bars and shadows
Where death has built a chair, hard and simple,
A future for itself.

Judy grins.
My armchair gives a jolt.

§

I leave the house,
A country I no longer love.

The moon advertises a better life.
One by one, streets and sleeping windows fall
Behind, arguments for and against.

I come to a fence, a wide tobacco field.
One light in a tenant shack,
Far on the other side.
A man with a cigarette perhaps,
Plotting a future, his lungs feeding on dreams
Of profit and loss.

§

The quarter moon
Smiles sharply at a life with others.

There's a point in Defoe's island book
Where Crusoe contemplates the reef and the new wreck
And realizes that one man's safety
Is another man's destruction.

Or an animal's perhaps.
The fox I shotgunned in the yard once: rabies,
A red plot against the snow, something or other.
That night I wasn't safe. Barely tamed,
My hands lay like animals at my sides.

§

Judy's foster mother begged
He be kept alive and studied....

The smallest cells, lethal genes, the secret
Circuitry of his behavior
All beg to be understood.

The night's electric blue.
                        Past Saturn
A probe moves us to the fringes of what we know.

I stand here watching the light in that shack.
Everything is reduced to that one light,
Warm, yellow, alive, and oddly poignant
Across the field. Suddenly
There's darkness where it was.

HEAVEN

The mobiles he made of broken pane-
Glass, tin, or brass piping
Always touched off tunes
Under the front and back porch eaves.

Every tree had a house for the right bird.
Gourds for purple martins
Hung from a wire between distant trees
And looked like whole notes against the sky.

The cellar was where he did his making.
I learned to size nails, love the everlasting balm
Of paint, the clean scent of soft pine
And sanded oak, the good smell of sweat,
The look of sawdust
Like a pile of gold filings under his vise.

My mother gone, he quit the church, after years of Mass.
But the brass touchings of his chimes
Are matins that take me
Through the cold crisis of waking
Moment by moment.
Sawdust is a sermon.
Birdcries are *Kyries*.
My father built a heaven about my ears.

II

TOWARD PARIS

My first time on the night train
I couldn't sleep

With expectation, the lucky
Shapes of houses wrapped in dream—

Trees slowed, then creaked to a stop.
4:00 a.m. under country stars.

Lower the window: new air,
A deserted dirt road and

A peasant pedalling away,
A wand-like loaf in his hand,

Tail-light growing weak
Red in the dark, as if his work

Was to bring fresh light
To woods and fields. He did,

Keeping me there at that
Balanced blue hour even later

In the Sainte Chappelle,
The blur of the Louvre and after.

HISTORIC PRESENT

(Loire Valley, 1975)

Blois, Chambord, Amboise, and then
The road again, distance
Arranging scenes in the windshield.

God, let something astonishing arrive
To erase sharp words,
The Peugeot's flat, a son's anger.

Dates, the mythic details
Of famous lives, fact and motive
Ask for mastery, promise answers

That down the road might matter.
De Medici, De Guise, François I—
Who did what to whom and when

In these regal but impossible plots?
Only the general suffices:
Power, jealousy, betrayal of love.

A wife and son ice me with looks.
Once wanted, information taunts like
Royal emblems—boar and porcupine:

Ne me touchez pas. And the rain
Relents, as if ordered, giving us
A night in some small town, nameless now.

After dinner my family goes to bed.
I take a walk, too full
Of good food and helpless history.

Who was it, freshly stuffed with truffles,
Went to see Huguenots
Dance themselves blue in the noose?

I even forget where da Vinci died, but
Never this summer night,
Nor the crimson heart of poppies

Blooming along a path that stops dead
At the riverbank and turns inward:
I see a palace chamber, an open casement

Brilliant with moonlight, a poster bed.
My queen, my young blond prince
Still sleep in this fragile light.

—

VALLURIS: CAFÉ DES VOYAGEURS

At red metal tables
We rest outside over beers
And appraise what we've seen
In the low slanting light.
There are palm trees,
But this is no paradise.
The past is expensive.
Our legs are dumb from walking.
A blue wall protects us
From a wind as stubborn as want.

Our son climbs
With a dark-haired boy
On the plinth of the "Goat-herd"
That Picasso made for the square.
They hug its bronze legs
And turn about
Where merchants on Sunday morning
Pile the newspaper
To wrap their flowers and fish—
A fresh indifference to art,
To dates in the *Michelin*,
And the Roman ruins nearby.

Running and laughing,
Our son chases pigeons again.
They land and scatter.
We watch them circle,
Gust in the wind
Over roofs tilting
Toward some other haven,
Something lost
Always longing
To be found.

SKIING AT VALLOIRE

With lips bunched as if to kiss,
He lowers the Luger, this SS man,
And blasts me from sleep to the floor,

My tongue pleading with the dark,
Until it catches the cold room,
Steadies my breath.

§

They came to this village
To hunt the Maquis. Decades ago.
But at 3:00 a.m., if I close my eyes,
That footage stutters to life:

I can't escape, gloved knuckles
Hammering the door, gutteral shouts,
Families shoved to the square—
Stories I heard in the bar tonight
From a haunted old man in his cups.

§

Sleep is already a winner:
    Trained by uniforms, we kneel,
The pit we dug waiting,
    The last sacrament coming down
The skeletal line one crack at a time,
    The kapo with something,
Said the old man, like a paten
    To protect the officer's boots,
Telling in a wine-thick voice

How it was
Better at night, the shutters closed,
    To keep one from thinking.

§

Now light is leaking like hope through the louvers.
There's a good gong of bells for the Mass.
Peasants climb a dawn-blue hill to the church.
    One of them spat: *Putain boche, vive—*
A pistol report, the tumble of rags in a ditch.

§

The black pool
Of coffee is gone. Only hairline cracks
Inside the cup. My skis and boots
Stand by the door, orange and crayon blue,
Bright, like the colors of cheap toys
Or a life given back
In flashy historical weather.

⌐.

PERCHED VILLAGES, SAVOIE

Like aeries, they cling
To outcrop or cliff ledge.

They mock what passes below,
And the road that coils up reminds you,

Like life at the top,
Of the slow-moving snail and its shell.

Cobbles, a few cafés. Cold, pure
Water—a fountain where women wash clothes.

In the Middle Ages, they watched,
Swooped upon travellers: a tribute for passage.

Now they just watch.
One thin road runs out of sight

Around sheer rock walls: Finality
Broods, bongs

Out a question at noon.
You could find the priest,

Confess, live with old stones,
Pray for the rest of your life.

But the road pulls you down
In dizzy circles and the village

Rises higher and higher
Preparing an antique heaven at your back.

LEAVINGS

By itself on my desk, left this morning,
A big envelope, white, with bright Swiss stamps—
A summons

    To newspaper photos, a friend's face,
    Black-bordered tributes,
    A few gift sketches and prints, words
    From his widow trying to explain.

I turn to the window, something
To keep the news at bay, or slowly let it in:

    Mean sky, black pecan
    Like one of his sketches—
    A wild dark weave of branches
    Nubbed with nuts
    No longer alive
    But clinging.

§

Last summer, just there,
By the augered pecan, in the live shade,
Dressed in white, he stood for a photo.

    But this is the wrong end of summer,
    And not wanting to,
    I see him at the wrong end of a rifle
    And freeze.

§

This evening, over a half-eaten meal,
I look out again on the tree
That he sketched, and taught me to see.

How easily it lets go its leaves,
Keeps a pose, adjusts to the heavy gray
Between branches
Mined with buds.

Mined with old conversation:
Gravity and Grace. Heaviness
Was all he had at the end.

§

Days later, the sky
Is low, thick-spread, impasted with a knife,
The driveway
Looking-glass slick, a last place for leaves.

With a young wife, a son the same age
As mine, dressed in white, racket in hand,
In the threshing shade, he waits

Like the envelope on my desk:
Une sensibilité de peau de fleur, a eulogy says
And he hovers here, there, to tell me
I'm nut hard, American to the core.

§

And his closest friend was a priest.
It's matins and hard hours, a skeletal tree.
A figure prone in the snow. Skypane opaque.

Not like the Alps, blue above
The studio at Sommet de Vignes
Where all that beauty,
Refusing canvas,
Failed.

And only failures teach, he thought.
Those who can, do—the rest is in the clippings,
The phrase, "se donna la mort,"
A euphemistic *passé simple*
That's never simple.

    A cardinal flies to the tree,
    Sits like a red memory.

§

Back from the A&P
With bagsful of dull pains,
I park the car, sit with the friend-
Ship of an old song

    And the tree looms up
    Printed by a Hunter's Moon,
    A pen-and-ink on the white
    Clapboard wall.

When I turn on the top back step
And see the tree hugging its shadow, I know
He's still there.

§

A cold has burned us for days.
Our cat's balled up at the base of the tree.
No lust for the hunt.
The grass, Rembrandt brown.

    A teacher,
    He shows me how to look at the dark givens;
    He paints the leaves away and

Leaves the burst pods that don't quite fall
But petal out into the black flowers
On a white page:

See how it drinks up the light
How its shadow fattens in the grass
And the dead nuts cling.
See, black and helpless as a phone-pole.
Twigs bleed rain and the shadow grows.
Mine seduced me on a Brittany beach
I came to paint. Rocks and a burning blue simplicity
Brought me to tears: "Trop beau, trop fort."
Did I mean something else I couldn't bear?
Being sportif didn't help, the fullback neck
You said I had. . . .

§

Journées mortelles—
That given phrase hunts me through colorless hours
Until late in the west when it brightens,
The bottom spilling
                    Yellow light
Like a brown bag suddenly breaking,
                              Dropping
A liquid sun
            And sunspears that might simply kill
If I couldn't catch, hold, and give them back.

In memory of Jean-Claude Rouiller

NAVAJO LAND

Hogans and beat-up trucks,
roadside ramadas,
dustdevils, sandstone and silence.
And between the canyon rims
it's wall to wall blue overhead,
the same bits of sky
you see on the belts,
fingers, and necks of these first people.

High in the desert
under such a wide sky,
there are no small moments.
In dry air hot as a sauna
that pigmy juniper
might as well be a redwood.
And the sun
is a fiery spider
knitting its filaments
as in the Anasazi petroglyph
we saw from horseback
at the trailhead.
Oblivion has not yet seen to them,
these "old ones,"
and next to a tongue
of soot from a campfire
in the tenth century
we see their thoughts
figured in stone—
hand, lizard, scorpion, deer—
reminders of a seeing so pure
it begs for rebirth.
But this is romance too.
My native guide,
more up to date than I,

more interested in Larry Bird
and the NBA
than the ancient quail
carved in the sandstone
above his horse,
wants to trade
turquoise and silver
for a Celtic's hat
with a plastic adjustable band.

§

We hike
to the beds of dinosaurs
where scholars came to read the bones
and puzzle out the body
architecture of great animals
gone but for the three-toed prints
that lope to the edge of the canyon rim
and into the deep dry air,
prints made too long ago even to imagine
or make sense of,
but later at a skeletal ramada
I see how we make what we need—
silver, turquoise and jade,
jewelry on velvet black as a wild night sky
above the mesa.

A raven floats over.
"Nothing around here," says the Indian boy,
"but rattlers and jackrabbits."

And the ageless glyphs of the Anasazi:
*sun, quail, spider,
scorpion, turtle, deer....*

⌒

RAVEN, MOUNTAIN, SNOW

The after-Christmas blue
Of snow in high country, our cabin
Broken into and looted, ravens
In the Ponderosa, a mocking crew.

Glass swept, I work my way
Along the mesa rim on a snow crust
That breaks and puts me up to my waist
In the mockery of ravens again.

And the three distant peaks,
Mountains first sacred to the Hopi,
Are scarred with ski runs
Clear-cut through fir and spruce.

But the air is cold and pure.
And all the Zen props are in place—
Mountain, snow, and pine—
To remind me

Of the Rinpoche to the novice:
You must place a ladder
Against the pear tree
So the thief won't break his leg.

Three heavy ravens give up,
Caw less at the nothing I need to flee.
Rung by rung, afternoon descends
In the bright fading colors of a bruise.

OUT AND BACK

Monks will say it's want that fogs the glass,
But that's what moves you through the inlet

Against the tide—instead of away from your body
To a vision empty and free—where you lift and

Settle with soft heaves of the sea, looking back
To a landfall line of toylike summer homes,

To a bowl of sky and a simple circle of sun
That some child in you might have wanted to draw,

Before you drift out, floating above yourself,
Looking down, the boat a white bobbing shoe,

Your sweatshirt a red spot at the vanishing point
When a Yellowfin takes your bait with a great leap,

And runs, the reel keening with drag,
But less and less, as you bring him back

And yourself to the old gaff and the red colors
Of what you must always return to.

TAR RIVER AGAIN

The afternoon drifts away on the river,
Taking me downstream toward my father again.

It's a twelve mile meander from Falkland,
And after rain, you just drag a paddle to steer.

The water is fast asleep, glossy and pulling.
Treeshades, solid as trees, want to bar the way,

But I see him again, slowly lowered into earthsleep,
And this bed of bright pebbles no longer astounds.

Two turtles slip from a log. A cardinal darts
From a bush, like a heart that made it green.

I want the end to elude me, but water pulls us on,
Back where we saw an egret standing on its image.

I ache for that perfect campsite, high on the bank,
And dream it as soon as we pass on that last day

Of heaven. Our fire ebbs in a stone ring.
We hear an owl hoot, a hound baying in the distance

As we ready ourselves for the night. Already
I miss him, so for once I inflate his blue mattress,

And love to think of him drifting, buoyed toward sleep
On my breath. In this way, always, I softly let us down.

⌣

III

THE SUNKEN LIGHTSHIP
OFF FRYING PAN SHOALS

On a weekend you could follow
Boats with Lorans and fancy electronics,
    But that's too easy, crowded,
And says nothing for the unseen
      That wants you to find it alone,
      Says: Take the seaward channel
Under the bridge, under cars that lull hundreds
        To sleepy work
          Over the metal grid that endlessly keens
On a weekday morning between seven and nine.

Scuttled at the end of the war,
    Eighty feet down,
Eighteen nautical miles southeast of the inlet,
Landfall just out of sight—
      That old guy at the boatyard saying,
It's where king mackerel school up in October.

You'd never make for this place on a whim.
Not for some tourist
    Notion of freedom
      Or romance of the open sea
Would you squint the inlet
    Alone on a flood tide
      With wind stiff at your back,
But you might venture out on compass and luck
    For an old need
      The way those wooden-hulled captains did.

At Pinfish Point,
You wait with a throw net and watch
    A heron hunt in the reeds
        Until gulls converge,
Falling upon mullet in mid-channel,
    The whole green portside surface
        Sown with darts of spray.

    Bait poached from the gulls,
Well-hatch tight and deck secure,
    You gulp at the air
        And ready yourself
For tons of tide driving in the narrows,
Then slam,
    Punch and bang your way
        Past the Army Dredger,
Now puffing like a Lawn Boy in the distance astern,
Spewing bottom from its shunt pipe
As if it could tame the inlet forever.

130 degrees southeast
There's nothing but horizon
    And sun lifting itself
        From the heaving glitter.
You try to needle the heading,
Not as easy as finding First Savings and Loan,
    But you follow the old guy's lead:
        When the island's two towers
    Have inched together and sit
On the first and fourth knuckle of your fist,
    Keep going until everything's gone.
Then skin an eye for signs on the surface.

    You kill the engine
    And let *dead in the water*
Mean something else for a change—
    The boat's right wisdom for drift.
Any moment could prove that you're here,

The lightship working in a different way,
        An imaginary skull
Grinning in a gangway below at anyone
        Who would want to be saved, or think
That years from now this solo trip might matter
        More than the moment itself enlarged
By the good that will follow your first line,
        The dorsal-hooked bluefish that flashes
        Once and is gone.

Space means promise and loss.
Two pelicans crash in a corkscrew dive,
        Come up empty
        With long apologetic looks,
Then labor aloft.

You coax things, hum to the sky.
        The clouds now seem to respond,
Slide your reflected face from the surface
        And you see below,
        Deep for the first time:
Millions of glass-minnows moving in unison,
        Now raining up
And away from the reaping mouths of bonito
That slash the surface like dozens of sickles.
        Now, splashes,
        The shriek of gulls,
        The reel gone mad,
Its line flying until you haul back,
And feel it heavy and alive with the moment,
As you gain,
        Then lose,
Then slowly gain,
Anxious for the slow-coming
        Shape and flash
Of what you might leave the lightship with.

PHANTOMS AT SWAN QUARTER

There is nothing old in America save the forests . . .
that is, in itself, worth many a monument and
ancestor.
                                    —CHATEAUBRIAND

All through the inside weather of winter, our storms
        And freezes, I fold, unfold the chart,
An eye to the pale blue seas at sister islands
        That want us to find what is there.

We chug through a maze of brushy meanders.
        Noon heat and the motor's threat
Send a moccasin from its eelgrass blind—a watery
        Cursive that says it was here.

Past the barnacled carcass of an oyster boat,
        The water opens a smooth new sheet.
We pick up speed on a dead reckon across the bay,
        Red nuns nodding astern

As now we make for the Judith Narrows, veering
        From an Ocracoke ferry that falls
To port, its bridge above the marsh grass fading
        Like a French cathedral in favor

Of the first bars of an unknown bird that takes
        The place of the motor when I kill it.
But the bird flees, hides a shy blue before our book
        Can give it a name. An osprey whistles

And dives, redwings flit through cattails, stronger
        For their whispered names. On cushions
We stretch out, yield to a current, let our bodies
        Play Adam and Eve, taste the deep salt,

Feel the hot-towel press of the sun—witness
  Our only act. Bread, good brie,
A bottle of white Papillion. Even the landmark
  Tower, red across the bay, won't quite

Become a nick on the wide water under clouds
  That invent themselves, billow,
And darken. Light is never the same. Brown rays,
  Mating, fin the surface like sharks

As they circle, then bank in formation, delta wings
  In the clear water under the boat before
Three olive Phantoms streak in, screaming at wargames
  So low we see helmets that give us

The high sign and send every bird in the refuge
  Clattering up to darken the air
Like battle smoke, the settlement slow and sadly changed,
  With an old fear of the motor

Not starting, the squall quickly on us. Or the dream
  Motor starting on its own, dragging us back
Into winter, with no memory, only the map, the blues
  Fading, as if we had never been here.

SOUND BUOY

It presides
Over our passing
   In and out
Of the Bogue Narrows.
   We rise
From sea gullies
And watch it sway
To a mindless
Humping of waves.

In soft seas
   Its moans
Are more our own.
If I name it
Red Nun of the Narrows,
The pleasure won't last,
For it turns unruly at a whim
And will outlast our coming
   And going.

Once, alone,
In wild weather,
   I felt
The wallow and topple,
The fit of its color
In close thrashes,
   My tongue
Salted and stunned
Into a silence
That burned.

HOLE IN THE WALL

Salvation is consenting to die.
                    —SIMONE WEIL

1956

To get there we bike along the river
Until tar gives way
To a clam-shell road by charter boats,
Hanging nets, and the white gull-ripped air,
The road narrowing
By wild roses, curving, then there it is:
That dark tunnel under railroad tracks
Where, as if through a telescope,
The sea plays flash and dazzle
Beyond the smell of piss and creosote.
      Going through,
      I hold my breath

As I do when we dive from the top of the trestle,
Surfacing behind an old bridge pier in midstream,
Hidden, bursting with our black joke,
So that guys on shore panic to save us,
If they aren't drunk
And chance to notice we never come up.

1988

After a late call from an old friend,
The kind of news that grows more frequent,
And familiar, I leave my desk
And walk through a door
In the night, breathing the cool
Dark deeply to calm myself,
Finally becoming quiet as the sleeping house.
In the backyard, I look up at my lamplit room.

At the Hole In The Wall, friends,
If they beat you to the tunnel,
Became sudden silhouettes
Straining toward a light that could kill.

1958

Though none of us will actually die, not now,
We could, what with those riptides and trains,
Which is why only mongrel kids
Or guys with tattoos and bagged bottles
Would call it their beach, just beyond the town line
Where even the cops won't bother,
    Unless our Acapulco plunges
    Piss off the bridgekeep.
It's where we learn *cunt* and *fuck*,
Different words for dying, and watch
Punky make time stop
Behind the railroad shack
On top of Angie,
A cicada screaming for air.

1988

This morning,
At sunrise, through a wall of mist
I ride the ebbtide under the bridge,
Gulls screeching by the head boats,
And bang through the black water of Bogue Narrows,
The hull slamming less and less, as the sun,
a red circle, lifts above the heave and wallow
Into a brilliant moment that lasts the day,
Wordless and not suffering
From syntax, not once,
But haunted all the while by figures of light:

Winter Sunday nights,
Returning from a visit to the farm,
My mother and I wait in the car
And watch my father make a tunnel of the dark,
His breath a momentary phosphor,
Until the light comes on,
A hole that always looks ahead to the past.

⸺

BLUEFISHING THE BOGUE NARROWS

When weather couldn't be worse,
They school up thick in the inlet,
A fifty foot shrimper dropping from sight,
Then surging sky high on a swell,
Its twin screws twirling
The air like momentary pinwheels
In this neck unregenerate as ever.

If you can learn to ride the rip,
The steep chop and churn of the narrows—
Your deck-monkey friend at the rods
And you at the throttle ready for the rogue wave
That wants to send you pitchpoling under—
You can fill up that fishbox
In less than an hour.

Even seasoned boatmen
Have been scuttled by crosscurrents,
Taking it bow and stern
Until panic sent them for a final swim
In these wild waters
Where we test the fabric of dreams,
Discover what we've always known,
Why others fish ponds
Or snooze in the shade of a pier.

⌐

SKUNK FLAG

Fly it into port
And you're quick bait
For the guys already drunk
Under emblems of king and cobia
Fluttering from a stanchion
Or T-top antenna,
The hot air so detailed with epic success
That you finally understand
The only difference between a fairy tale
And a fish tale is
Once upon a time....

No other boats in sight,
I turned off the radio to be more alone
With someone recently gone.

A sea robin flickered, skimmed,
And re-entered with barely a splash.
The sea surface glittered.
The afternoon went on like that—
Nothing, not one strike.
Finally, I spilled my live bait over the side.

Later, at the house, I gazed out the window.
Distance overcome.
Skunked.
But beyond the pane, a hooded gull
Tilted and tacked down a channel of air,
Hovered, then folded its wings
Into awkward weight, stood on top
Of the walkway rail, still,
As if carved of wood and nailed in place—
An emblem of something given, beheld,
And not simply caught.

EAST OF CAPE FEAR

Doldrums.
The sea hasn't heaved
In an hour, the offing
Empty—
But they have
A way of appearing
Almost from inside
To rub an otherness
We seldom touch.

And before the fear
That makes the black fin
Always for a moment a shark,
They're here, breaching,
Two, three, four,
Dozens of buddha smiles
Around the boat in easy leaps,
Dives, and rolls before a last
Playful slap of flukes.

Far off, backlit by the sun,
Blow holes sprouting
Brilliant shrubs of mist,
They recede but still ride
The waves of our breath.

CAMELLIA

These buds,
Arranged in a hand-painted bowl,
Open faster it seems
Than on time-lapse film.
Bright trumpets, reminders—
Seven years south and I'm still taken
By that fine white defiance of December.

"Japonica" is its other name from a far
Country of pagodas and
Monks who saw the same blooms
As emblems of graceful awareness
And anonymously brushed them
With practiced lack of desire
Onto rice paper ages ago.

There is nothing slow, oriental here,
The white flower not inner
As I might like others to think. Self-
Interest speckles the white.

Late one night,
Dropping petals, one blossom was a mind
Bewildered, tired of love,
Each petal
A name fallen into the sad grave of sleep.
Listen to its whispers.

Stop, sleep, leave for work.
Brush the fallen petals from table to palm
And outside open that fist.
One by one, perfectly,
See how they lift, swirl up in a soft new wind,
Something neglected
But undeniably found.
Call it gladness, in spite of myself.

PASSAGE

Let me begin with a photo
Of a porch-swing
And a man in profile
Squinting toward the hillcrest—
Everything uneasily familiar,
The man a father
Just swinging,
Retired with a book
And a cup of tea.

Tuesday or Thursday, just before two,
He'll put down the book
Or the cup, waiting as always
For her
To crest the hill,
Then plunge, her body flickering
With sunshafts as she swerves
A red skateboard
On the gathered wave of the hill.

Under the arch of maple limbs,
She dips, ramps the drive
And launches herself into air—
Air that drains from the lungs
Of the man on the porch
As her auburn hair goes down
In flames behind the privet hedge
With a cry muted by distance
That might be his own
Mouth startled open, cup stalled
Inches from its saucer.

Her head lifts
Above the hedge, as if
From behind a dressing screen,
Then falls again.
It's Tuesday
And on Tuesday and Thursday
He expects
Her beauty to control
The difficult hill
That drops to an afternoon class,
Falls away
Like the cup and book
When up he heaves
And down the stairs
As fast as he can
He goes.

Flustered, she waves him off.
Okay, she says, wobbling,
Unsteady toward poise,
Picking up speed,
Taking the bright burn
On her thigh into hiding.
He watches her become small
With distance and depth.

A yellow leaf comes down.
A squirrel chirrs.
The sidewalk is empty,
Broken, and a concrete slab,
Jacked up by a maple root,
Is like the lid
Of an underground vault.
He turns to the porch
From the burden
Of what can happen
On any afternoon.

LISTEN

What my mother said would happen
If I didn't listen,

Has: she's standing right there,
Backlit by the west window,

Describing Molly, a parrot
That perches years from here—

An apartment over a tavern
I have never seen,

Hard by the river
She seems to stare at,

Seeing again that green bird
Full of squawk and jabber

Reeled into April rain
With a clothesline pulley.

And I know what's coming—
Her father's bar pal

Staggering into the stand,
The heavy cage falling

On top of a bird
That colored her girlhood.

But somehow I did listen,
And clearly see that cage,

An empty bell of black wire
Tolling this winter light.

SLEEP MOTHER

You never learned how, so I'm driving again,
Our headlights pushing back the desert dark.
A saguaro looms like a penitent on the fringe.

We are not going to Mass at the Spanish mission.
We are simply going and will never arrive.
The road forgets itself in the rearview

And you do something I have always wanted:
You take hold of one of my hands and resume
The broken story of your mother and father.

At last you can speak freely, as you just have.
The self-important moon is going down.
Just the story and my questions, our mingled voices,

As I adjust the speed, use highbeams and low.
Like musicians, we are able to listen, awake
To each other, the dark like a blessing that lasts.

—.

PART OF A STORY

Outside that predawn diner
Was a moment
Outside every moment I ever spent
With my father on that truck.
Bird voices, soft as honey,
Dropped through leaves in the dark.
Listen, he said,
To what he first heard on the farm,
Some story told by his mother.
But I ached to be old
Enough to be a driver like him
Awake while the world slept,
Tough enough to glug down coffee, hot,
And make the waitress laugh
With stories of my own.

What was that story
About doves, their sorrowful
Notes falling like ripe fruit?
I forget.
I forget everything
But us being outside
And his being outside
Of himself and taking time
To tell it in the quiet
While the hard hours
Of blacktop waited, me
Getting antsy for speed
And a chance to drive,
The east getting brassy already.

These many years later,
Up before dawn
With the trucker I wanted to be,
The dark dream fading,
I wait for the coffee to perk,
On the way to my desk, that dove
Mourning outside in the eaves,
Across the years to another
Above the distant wheeze
Of deisels idling
Dark under trees.

PHOTO EXHIBIT

There was a farmhouse
Snowbound and, though in color,
Mostly white. I stood in the road
By the slatted red snowfence.

The house was deep in a field,
Empty, guarded by one huge hemlock.
It had a ruined garden with beige stubble
And a weathered wooden gate

I could have entered,
But my son tugged at my loose right hand.
Outside, August blazed. People lost eyes
On the sidewalk, doubled in glass,

Warped and melted on fenders.
Horns honked and buildings swayed
In the heat. I found our car, packed us in,
And drove toward that snowbound farm.

—

REFLECTIONS ON A LIKENESS OF LUKE

Ceci n'est pas une pipe.
—RÉNÉ MAGRITTE

This isn't Luke.
It reveals an obsession with Luke.

Luke had a mole, right here.
This is Luke.

It's a dream image of Luke.
It's Luke dreaming of a better image.

It shows a shotgun, not a guitar.
It's the guy who robbed the Zip Mart.

It shows the Luke in all of us.
It's a Luke-type look-alike, kind of.

It's a mask haunted by others.
It's the lonely self haunted by its own mask.

It's a woman posing as Luke.
It's Luke posing as himself, unsuccessfully.

This isn't Luke.
It's a lie that reveals the true Luke.

It's the only Luke of its kind.
It's more real, more knowable than Luke.

It's Luke mythologized.
It's Luke deconstructed.

It's happy and sad, deep and shallow—
It squints the viewer, reads the reader.

ACKNOWLEDGEMENTS

Grateful acknowledgement is made to the editors of the following publications in which these poems or earlier versions of them originally appeared:

The American Scholar: "Dark Preface."
The Arts Journal: "Sailplane," "Toward Paris."
The Carleton Miscellany: "After Friends."
Calliope: "Sleep Mother."
Denver Quarterly: "Hole in the Wall."
The Georgia Review: "Equations."
The Gettysburg Review: "Skunk Flag," "Raven, Mountain, Snow."
Kansas Quarterly: "Photo Exhibit."
The Laurel Review: "With My Father at Crow's Nest Cottage," "Skiing at Valloire," "The Sunken Lightship Off Frying Pan Shoals," "Reflections on a Likeness of Luke," "Heaven."
New England Review: "Stephen Judy's Execution."
The Journal: "Tar River Again," "Part of a Story."
The Ohio Review: "Backwaters."
Poet and Critic: "A Sense of the Other Side," "Bluefishing the Bogue Narrows," "Sound Buoy."
Poet Lore: "Phantoms at Swan Quarter."
Poetry Miscellany: "Camellia."
Poetry: "Feeders."
Poetry Northwest: "East of Cape Fear."
Prairie Schooner: "Leavings."
Quarterly West: "Perched Villages, Savoie."
Raccoon: "Story of a Sound."
River City: "Passage."
The Sewanee Review: "Brothers of the Double Life."
Shenandoah: "Catlight," "Answering Voices."
Southern Poetry Review: "Historic Present," "Navajo Land."
Stone Country: "Valluris: Café des Voyageurs."
The Texas Review: "Out and Back," "Listen."

"Dark Preface" was reprinted in *The Anthology of American Verse & Yearbook of American Poetry*, ed. Alan F. Pater (Monitor Press 1986/1987).

"Toward Paris," "Valluris: Café des Voyageurs," "Historic Present," "Skiing at Valloire," "Perched Villages, Savoie," "Leavings," and "Phantoms at Swan Quarter" were first collected and published with other poems as a chapbook entitled *Pilgrims* by Ampersand Press (1987).

⌐

PETER MAKUCK

Born in New London, Connecticut, in 1940, Peter Makuck received his B. A. from St. Francis College and a Ph.D. from Kent State University. Since 1975 he has taught at East Carolina University, where he is Professor of English and Editor of *Tar River Poetry*. In 1974–1975 he was a Fulbright Lecturer on modern American poetry at Université de Savoie, France, and in 1990 he was Visiting Professor of Creative Writing at Brigham Young University.

The author of a collection of short stories, *Breaking and Entering* (University of Illinois Press), Peter Makuck's first book of poems, *Where We Live*, with a Foreword by Louis Simpson, was published in 1982 by BOA Editions, Ltd.. Makuck has had poems and short stories published in *The Nation, Poetry, The Sewanee Review, The Virginia Quarterly Review,* and *The Georgia Review.* And his chapbook of poems, *Pilgrims* (Ampersand Press), was chosen by Pulitzer Prize winning poet Mary Oliver for the 1988 Brockman Award, which is given each year for the best collection of poetry by a North Carolinian. Peter Makuck currently resides in Greenville, North Carolina, with his wife, Phyllis, and their son, Keith.

BOA EDITIONS, LTD.
AMERICAN POETS CONTINUUM SERIES

Vol. 1 *The Führer Bunker:*
          A Cycle of Poems in Progress
          W. D. Snodgrass
Vol. 2 *She*
          M. L. Rosenthal
Vol. 3 *Living With Distance*
          Ralph J. Mills, Jr.
Vol. 4 *Not Just Any Death*
          Michael Waters
Vol. 5 *That Was Then:*
          New and Selected Poems
          Isabella Gardner
Vol. 6 *Things That Happen*
          Where There Aren't Any People
          William Stafford
Vol. 7 *The Bridge of Change:*
          Poems 1974–1980
          John Logan
Vol. 8 *Signatures*
          Joseph Stroud
Vol. 9 *People Live Here:*
          Selected Poems 1949–1983
          Louis Simpson
Vol. 10 *Yin*
          Carolyn Kizer
Vol. 11 *Duhamel:*
          Ideas of Order in Little Canada
          Bill Tremblay
Vol. 12 *Seeing It Was So*
          Anthony Piccione
Vol. 13 *Hyam Plutzik: The Collected Poems*
Vol. 14 *Good Woman:*
          Poems and a Memoir 1969–1980
          Lucille Clifton
Vol. 15 *Next: New Poems*
          Lucille Clifton
Vol. 16 *Roxa: Voices of the Culver Family*
          William B. Patrick
Vol. 17 *John Logan: The Collected Poems*
Vol. 18 *Isabella Gardner: The Collected Poems*
Vol. 19 *The Sunken Lightship*
          Peter Makuck